MEGA
Machines

By Deborah Lock

LONDON, NEW YORK, MUNICH,
MELBOURNE, AND DELHI

DK LONDON
Series Editor Deborah Lock
Project Art Editor Hoa Luc
Producers, Pre-production
Francesca Wardell, Vikki Nousiainen
Illustrator Hoa Luc

DK DELHI
Editor Pomona Zaheer
Assistant Art Editor Yamini Panwar
DTP Designers Anita Yadav,
Syed Md Farhan
Picture Researcher Sumedha Chopra
Dy. Managing Editor Soma B. Chowdhury

Reading Consultant Shirley Bickler

First published in Great Britain by
Dorling Kindersley Limited
80 Strand, London, WC2R 0RL

Copyright © 2014 Dorling Kindersley Limited
A Penguin Random House Company

10 9 8 7 6 5 4 3 2 1

001—253411—June/2014

A CIP catalogue record for this book is available from the British Library.

ISBN: 978-1-4093-5184-9

Printed and bound in China by South China Printing Company.

The publisher would like to thank the following for their kind permission
to reproduce their photographs:
(Key: a-above; b-below/bottom; c-centre; f-far; l-left; r-right; t-top)
1 Alamy Images: Zoonar / Yordan Rusev (bc). Dreamstime.com: Brad Calkins (Bbackground). 4–5 Alamy Images:
Gareth Byrne (t). 5 Dreamstime.com: Mark Sykes (bc). 6 123RF.com: scusi (tl). Dreamstime.com: Djburrill (bl).
6–7 Dreamstime.com: Matthewennisphotography (bc). 7 Dreamstime.com: Alex Ciopata (b); Djburrill (br).
8 Dreamstime.com: Djburrill (bl). 9 Alamy Images: David J. Green – work themes. Dreamstime.com: Djburrill (br).
10 Dreamstime.com: Djburrill (bl). 10–11 Alamy Images: Brandon Bourdages (c). 11 Dreamstime.com: Djburrill (br).
12 Dreamstime.com: Djburrill (bl). 13 Alamy Images: JG Photography (r). Dreamstime.com: Djburrill (br). 16 123RF.com:
scusi (tl). Dreamstime.com: Djburrill (bl). 17 Alamy Images: Zoonar / Yordan Rusev. Dreamstime.com: Djburrill (br).
18 Dreamstime.com: Djburrill (bl). 19 Alamy Images: StockPhotosArt – Industrial. Dreamstime.com: Djburrill (br).
20 Dreamstime.com: Djburrill (bl). 20–21 Alamy Images: Robert Davis. 21 Dreamstime.com: Djburrill (br). 24–25 Alamy
Images: dbtravel (b). 24 Dreamstime.com: Djburrill (bl). 25 Dreamstime.com: Djburrill (br). 26 123RF.com: Sabri Deniz
KIZIL (tl). Dreamstime.com: Djburrill (bl). 27 Alamy Images: Rjh_Catalog. Dreamstime.com: Djburrill (br).
28 Dreamstime.com: Djburrill (bl). 28–29 Alamy Images: RJH_CATALOG. 29 Dreamstime.com: Djburrill (br).
30 Dreamstime.com: Djburrill (bl). 31 Dreamstime.com: Djburrill (br). 32 Alamy Images: Vlad Breazu (cl); RJH_
CATALOG (tr). 33 Alamy Images: Conrad Elias (cr); pf (tl); Chris Madden (clb). 34 123RF.com: scusi (tl). Dreamstime.
com: Djburrill (bl). 35 Alamy Images: JoeFox / Radharc Images (b). Dreamstime.com: Djburrill (br). 36 Alamy Images:
Justin Kase z02z. Dreamstime.com: Djburrill (bl). 37 Corbis: Ocean (b). Dreamstime.com: Djburrill (br). 40 Alamy Images:
1bestofphoto (b). Dreamstime.com: Djburrill (bl). 40–41 Alamy Images: Zoonar / Yordan Rusev (bc). 41 Alamy Images:
Brandon Bourdages (b). Dreamstime.com: Djburrill (br). 42 Alamy Images: Gareth Byrne (t).
Jacket images: Front: Dreamstime.com: Jvdwolf (b), Uatp1 (tr).

All other images © Dorling Kindersley
For further information see: www.dkimages.com

Discover more at
www.dk.com

Contents

School Design Plan

30 m

25 m

Side of school | Front of school |

50 m

Scale

1 m =

Stage 1
Clearing the Site

"Hard hats on!"

says the Foreman, getting to work.

"Welcome to
the building site.
The plans are ready
for building a new school.
The mega machines are ready
to start work."

Rumble, rumble!

"Here they come!"

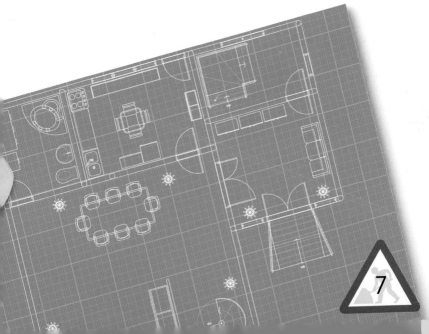

"What a mess!"

says the Foreman,
scratching his head.
The site is not level and
it is covered with rubble.
The bulldozer, front loader
and the dump truck
are needed.
The bulldozer pushes
the soil and rubble
with its blade.

It moves along
on crawler tracks.

Hum, rumble, hum!

The front loader scoops up
the mounds of soil and
rubble.
The bucket moves.

Forward…
down…

scoop...
up!

The front loader carries its loaded bucket raised high.

The dump truck will take
the soil and rubble away.
The bucket of the front loader
tips up over the dumping bed.

Swish, clatter,
clatter, swish!

The front loader goes
to and fro to collect
some more.

"Stage 1 is done,"

says the Foreman,
nodding his head.

The Busy Loader

This poem is about the movements of
a front loader. Say the poem aloud.
Make up some actions. Are you ready?

Rumble, rumble. Beep! Beep!

Scoop, lift, turn, tip!

Here's the busy loader.
Its big wheels
Rumble over the ground.

Pull the levers.
Lower down the bucket.
Scoop up the rubble.
Lift high the load.

Rumble, rumble. Beep! Beep!

Scoop, lift, turn, tip!

Here's the busy loader.
Its loaded bucket
High above the ground.

Pull the levers.
Turn over the bucket.
Tip out the rubble.
Out pours the load.

Rumble, rumble. Beep! Beep!

Scoop, lift, turn, tip!

15

Stage 2

Digging the Site

"What a noise!"

shouts the Foreman, covering his ears.

The site is now clear and the excavator has arrived.

The excavator is needed
to dig some deep holes.
The arm moves.

Lower... scoop...
lift... turn...
drop...
turn!

Whirr, rumble, whirr!

Along comes
the concrete mixer.
The mixing drum
must keep spinning.

"Pour the concrete
into the hole,"

orders the Foreman.

"Leave it
to harden."

More holes are
dug and filled.
This makes a firm base
for the new school.

19

The strong lorries bring the long pipes.
The backhoe digs out small trenches.
The builders lay the pipes into the trenches.

Lift... walk... lower... drop!

The loader covers the pipes with soil.
Water, gas and wire cables will go through these pipes.

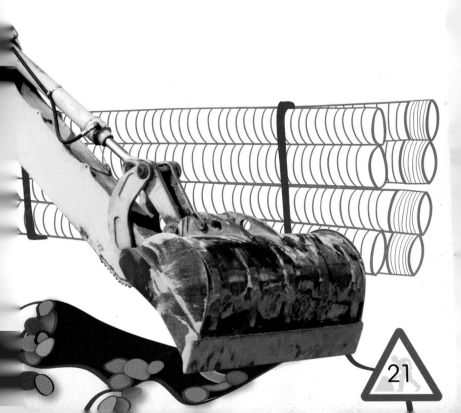

Backhoe Digger

bucket
This part digs out
the ground
to make trenches
and holes.

boom
This part moves
from side to side
and also moves
the dipper stick
and the bucket
up and down.

dipper stick

legs
This part keeps
the tractor steady.

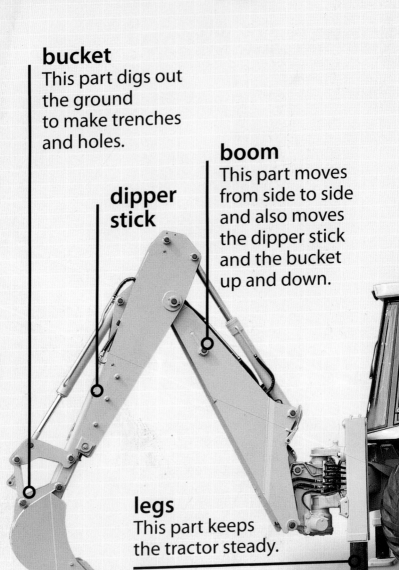

cab
This is the place where
the driver sits to drive
and control the boom
and the loader.

tractor
This is the part
with the power and
the wheels to move.

loader
This part is used
to lift and
move loads.

The concrete is hard.
The pipes have been laid.
The holes have been filled.
Here comes the roller
to make the ground
smooth and flat.

Roll, press, smooth!

The roller squashes down
the soil.

"Stage 2 is done,"
says the Foreman,
rubbing his ear.

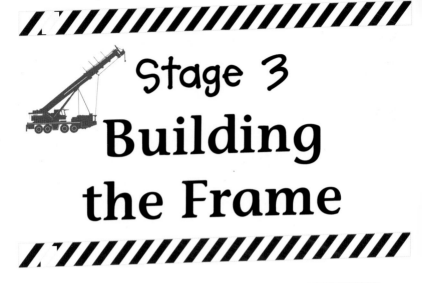

Stage 3
Building the Frame

"Raise the crane,"

shouts the Foreman, lifting his arms.

A large mobile crane arrives.

Up, up goes the boom.
The hook hangs from
the chain at the end
of the boom.

The long lorries bring
the strong steel girders.
The crane driver moves
the levers to lower the hook.

Lower... hook...
lift... turn...
lower... fit...
unhook!

The girders are picked up
one by one on the hook.

The upright girders
are fitted together first.
The crane swings
back and forth.

Other girders
are laid across.

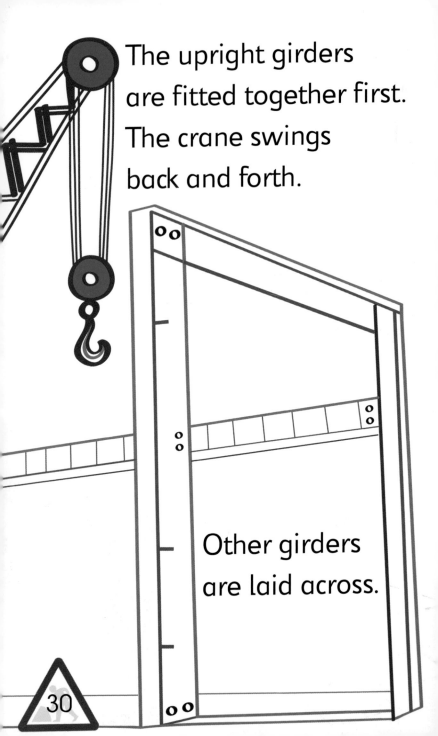

The girders will support
the floors and the roof
of the school.
The builders bolt the girders
together.

Turn, twist, hammer!

"Stage 3 is done,"

says the Foreman,
wiping his forehead.

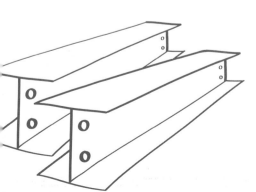

Cranes

There are many different types of cranes. Each type is useful for doing a different job.

Mobile tower crane

This crane can go along roads. It can reach up high over buildings.

Truck-mounted crane

This crane swings from side to side on the back of a truck to lift and move loads.

Sidelift crane

This crane is on a trailer and is used to load and unload containers.

Bulk-handling crane

This crane has a grabber to pick up and move bulky loads.

Tower cranes

These cranes are fixed into concrete on the ground. They are used for very tall buildings.

Stage 4
Finishing the School

"One month left,"

calls the Foreman, shaking his head. The huge lorries arrive with their heavy loads.

There are concrete blocks and white cladding for the walls, shiny windows and tall doors. The bricklayers spread the mortar and lay the blocks.

Builders are raised on
a truck-mounted lift.

The builders fit the cladding
onto the walls.
The vans arrive.
Here are the plasterer,
the decorator, the roofer,
the plumber, the electrician
and the carpenter to help.

"Two weeks left,"

shouts the Foreman,
rubbing his chin.

What is Everyone Doing?

Use these pictures to read about what everyone is doing to get the school ready.

door

carpet

light bulb

paintbrush

paint can

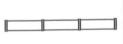
pipes

plug

red

hand basin

toilet

window

yellow

The decorator dips a into

the .

The walls are painted in

and .

The plumber lays the .

Each and is fitted.

The electrician wires sockets for each .

Every is fitted into the ceilings.

Each is rolled out and fitted.

Every is cleaned until it sparkles.

The carpenter fits every .

"One week left.
Let's work together."

shouts the Foreman,
checking the plans.
The lorries arrive with
the furniture.
Everyone helps to unload and
carry it all into the school.

"Stage 4 is done. Good job!"

says the Foreman.
The new school is finished.
The mega machines
rumble away.

Rumble, hum, rumble!

Grand School Opening

Friday 15th May at 11 o'clock

The Headteacher and Staff
welcome you to the Grand Opening of
Lower Hook School
by Mayor Sands

Join a tour of the school
Performances by
Lower Hook Brass Band
Lower Hook Singers

With thanks to Lower Hook Scouts
for sandwiches and drinks

Mega Machines Quiz

1. What are the mega machines building?

2. Which machine digs the deep holes?

3. Where does a driver sit on a machine?

4. What does the crane lift?

5. On what day and date did the school open?

Answers on page 45.

Glossary

cladding layer that protects the outside of a building

concrete mix of cement, sand, small stones and water

design drawing to look like a finished building or object

foreman someone who is in charge of the other workers

girder large strong steel beam used to make the frame of a building

site place where a new building is built

Index

Answers to the Mega Machines Quiz:
1. A school; **2.** An excavator;
3. In the cab; **4.** The girders;
5. Friday 15th May.

Guide for Parents

DK Reads is a three-level interactive reading adventure series for children, developing the habit of reading widely for both pleasure and information. These chapter books have an exciting main narrative interspersed with a range of reading genres to suit your child's reading ability, as required by the National Curriculum. Each book is designed to develop your child's reading skills, fluency, grammar awareness, and comprehension in order to build confidence and engagement when reading.

Ready for a *Beginning to Read* book

YOUR CHILD SHOULD

- be using phonics, including consonant blends, such as bl, gl and sm, to read unfamiliar words; and common word endings, such as plurals, ing, ed and ly.

- be using the storyline, illustrations and the grammar of a sentence to check and correct his/her own reading.

- be pausing briefly at commas, and for longer at full stops; and altering his/her expression to respond to question, exclamation and speech marks.

A VALUABLE AND SHARED READING EXPERIENCE

For many children, reading requires much effort but adult participation can make this both fun and easier. So here are a few tips on how to use this book with your child.

TIP 1 Check out the contents together before your child begins:

- read the text about the book on the back cover.

- read through and discuss the contents page together to heighten your child's interest and expectation.

- make use of unfamiliar or difficult words on the page in a brief discussion.

- chat about the non-fiction reading features used in the book, such as headings, captions, recipes, lists or charts.

TIP 2 Support your child as he/she reads the story pages:

- give the book to your child to read and turn the pages.

- where necessary, encourage your child to break a word into syllables, sound out each one and then flow the syllables together. Ask him/her to reread the sentence to check the meaning.

- when there's a question mark or an exclamation mark, encourage your child to vary his/her voice as he/she reads the sentence. Demonstrate how to do this if it is helpful.

TIP 3 Praise, share and chat:

- the factual pages tend to be more difficult than the story pages, and are designed to be shared with your child.

- ask questions about the text and the meaning of the words used. These help to develop comprehension skills and awareness of the language used.

A FEW ADDITIONAL TIPS

- Try and read together everyday. Little and often is best. These books are divided into manageable chapters for one reading session. However after 10 minutes, only keep going if your child wants to read on.

- Always encourage your child to have a go at reading difficult words by themselves. Praise any self-corrections, for example, "I like the way you sounded out that word and then changed the way you said it, to make sense."

- Read other books of different types to your child just for enjoyment and information.

Series consultant **Shirley Bickler** is a longtime advocate of carefully crafted, enthralling texts for young readers. Her LIFT initiative for infant teaching was the model for the National Literacy Strategy Literacy Hour, and she is co-author of *Book Bands for Guided Reading* published by Reading Recovery based at the Institute of Education.

Here are some other DK Reads you might enjoy.

Pirate Attack!
Come and join Captain Blackbeard and his pirate crew for an action-packed adventure on the high seas.

Deadly Dinosaurs
Roar! Thud! Meet Rexy, Sid, Deano and Sonia, the dinosaurs that come alive at night in the museum. Who do you think is the deadliest?

Playful Puppy
Holly's dream has come true – she's given her very own puppy. Although she tries to train him, share her delight in the playfulness of her new puppy.

Little Dolphin
Follow Little Dolphin's adventures when he leaves his mother and joins the older dolphins for the first time. Will he be strong enough to keep up?

Bugs Hide and Seek
Be surprised! Some bugs have the perfect shape and colour to stay hidden. They look like parts of the plants around them. Can you spot them?